Prepositions Made Easy

Language and Literacy

We Know This !

Vocabulary knowledge is the single most important aspect of oral English proficiency which in turn enhances student success with Academic Literacy.

Students do not need to master English grammar in the primary grades.

Students benefit from translations during English lessons.

Children at play participate in a great deal of social activity even with little or no common language. Communication exchanges may be non-linguistic vocalizations, pointing, nodding, gestures and pantomime. The activities in our English Module are games; students 'play' with each other and with specific English vocabulary.

Language education must begin as social interaction, and lessons must maintain that essence of communications.

Important

Students are not to work alone

on the following activity pages.

These worksheets are for instruction.

Use them for listening and speaking -

* point and say, to introduce/review

* say an object and have students point

* a student says for others to point

* to talk about items or show & tell

i.e., my _____ is yellow. I have a _____

* to copy the word under a picture

* to make a booklet and write a phrase

Prepositions

The easiest prepositions tell "where".
For example, in, out, under, over, beside, behind, between, outside, around,
in front of, up, down, through, across, off, towards, into, outside

Tell students that in English prepositions tell where. Introduce different prepositions later.

A prepositional phrase is a preposition with a noun. For example,
in the house, under the table, around the city, beside my friend

1. Start the lesson on prepositions by drawing a box. Place a finger
   in the box and say "in". Translate "in", and then repeat the word
   in English. Have students copy the box in their notebooks.

2. Draw a ball in the box. Say, "in, in the box". Students repeat.

3. Draw a car. Put somebody "in the car". Students must repeat.

4. Draw a house. Put somebody "in the house", in the tree,
   in my mouth, in my desk, in the bank, etc. Students repeat.

5. Continue with pictures and speaking. Ask students to suggest
   ideas. Write the prepositional phrases, in the box, etc.

6. Review the preposition the next day. See if students can point to
   the correct picture when you say it. This is a listening activity.

7. Next, ask students to say the prepositional phrase when you
   point to a drawing. This is a speaking exercise.

> Repeat the same activities for new prepositions.
> Hand out the preposition concept sheet.
> Translate each preposition.

Teaching with a Whiteboard

Make a clean copy of a topic picture page or review activity, scan it and add it as a new file on your computer.

Create a Whiteboard folder and move all the teaching sheet to it.

When you are presenting new vocabulary, move the file onto the whiteboard and the screen. Students will see it better and you will be able to focus student attention and learning better .

- You can also use it to label pictures/write in answers as students copy it onto their own paper copy.

- Review the vocabulary. Use a 'say it and point to it' activity using a single word, a riddle, a category, or a context phrase or sentence. i.e., pencil, yellow pencil, Where is my yellow pencil? What can you write with?

The activity also models the way that partners can play at their desks, which is a good way to practise for listening and speaking.

in

Basic Activity for Prepositions of Location

Use the form on the following page as a followup activity after introducing a preposition of location.

Students write the proposition word inside the oval.

Then they either draw or cut and paste examples of the preposition from magazines.

This form has multiple uses:

- use a color word instead of a preposition

- use an alphabet letter for phonics

- use for seasonal concepts

- use for categorizing
  i.e., wheels – car, bike, buggy, skateboard, etc.
      music - rap, jazz, pop, etc

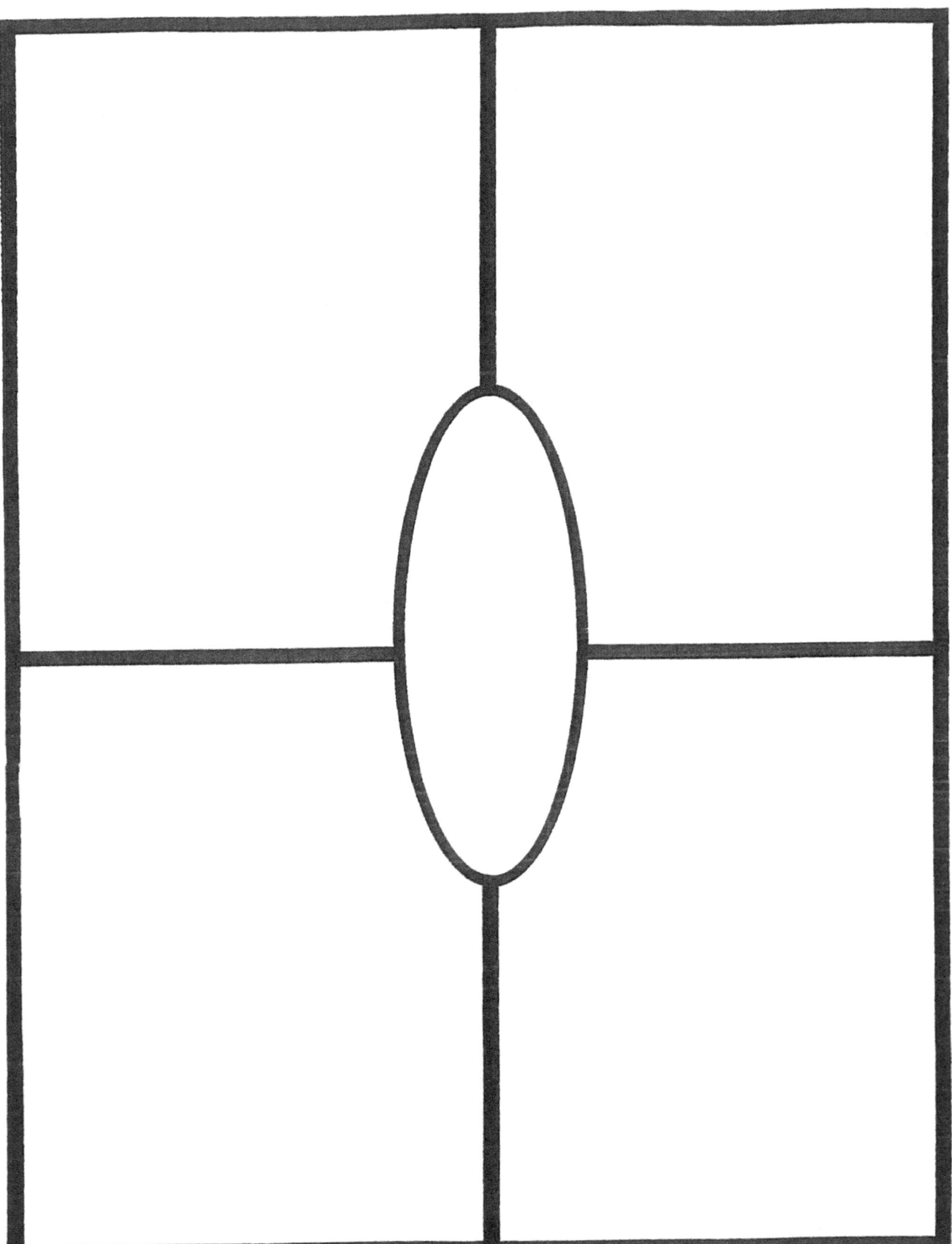

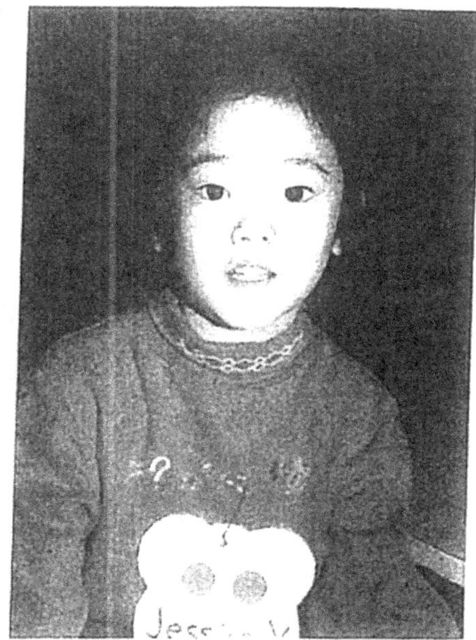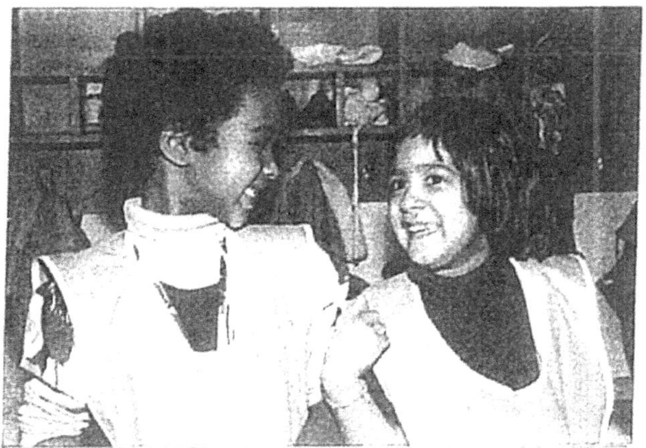

Inside the Egg

Read – Chickens Aren't the Only One
        by Ruth Heller K-5 (video URL below)
      - Guess What Is Growing Inside This Egg
        by Mia Posada K-5
      - An Egg is Quiet
        by Dianna Hutts Aston K-5 (video URL below)
      - What's Inside That Egg – K-3 Scholastic

Video - An Egg is Quiet

https://www.youtube.com/watch?v=KgVaNbrCayU

Video - Chickens Aren't the Only Ones

https://www.youtube.com/watch?v=zCEuoxje01k

Student Activities
- Make eggs all over an easel chart and fill them in as students brainstorm animals or insects born from eggs.

- Make a class book – students choose one of the ideas from the brainstorm activity or the books/videos and use the following form to illustrate one. The pictures are then stapled together into a class book and read to everyone.

What's in the Egg?

What's in the egg?

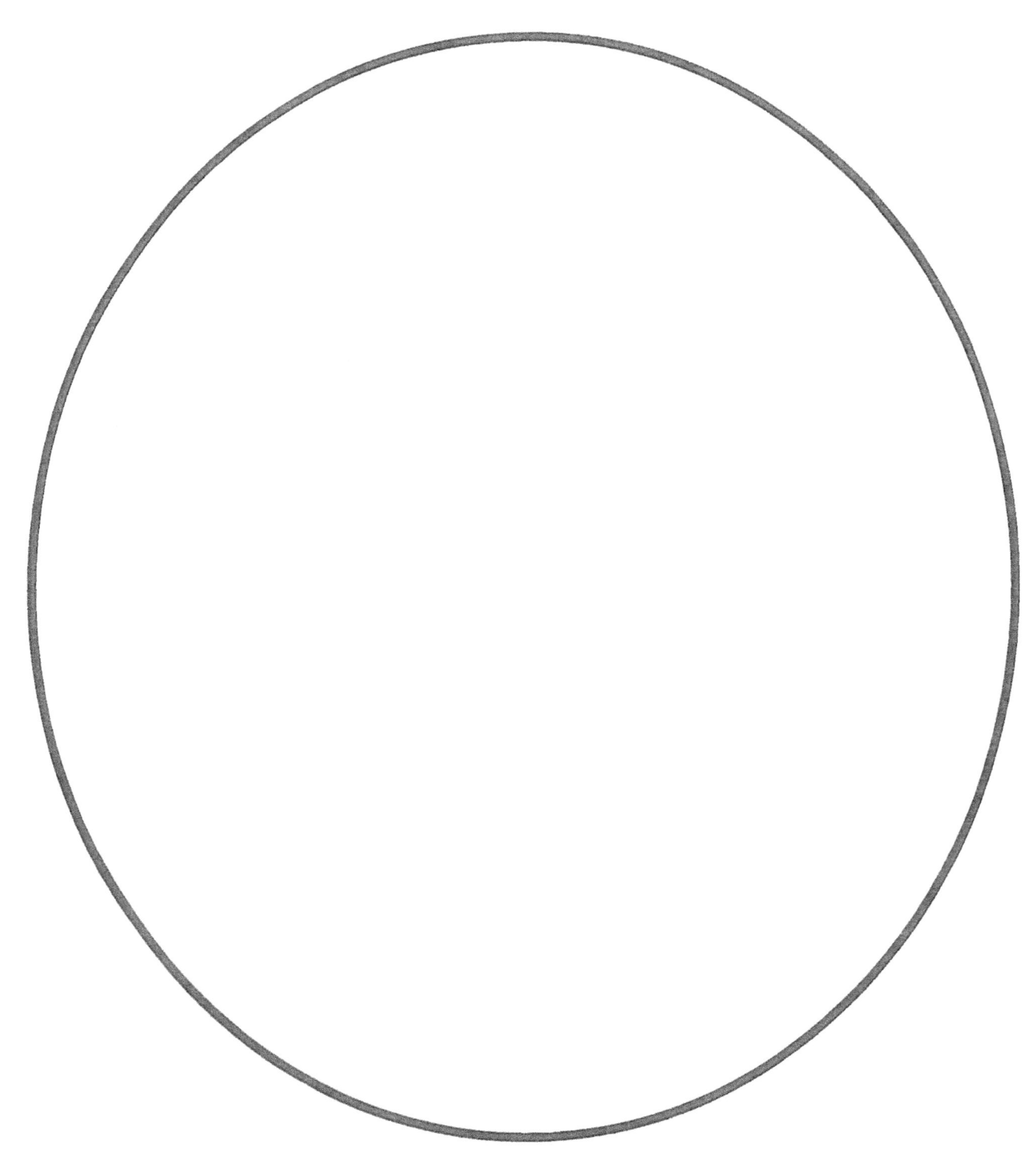

Preposition Activities
What's in that Box?

Students sign up to bring something to class and then to place it in 'the box' for others to guess.

It could be a shoe box or a moving box, a lunch box or a jewelry box, or basically anything in between.

This is similar to a show and tell activity since students guess what's in the box by asking questions.

Alternatively, the teacher could have a variety of box sizes, and place something in each one that reviews vocabulary items from the unit that students are studying.

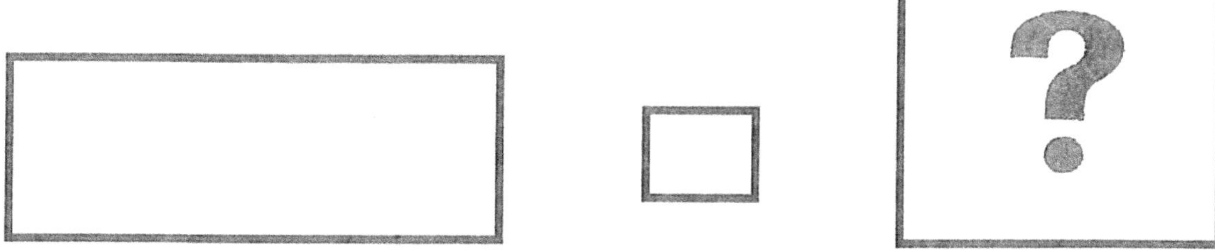

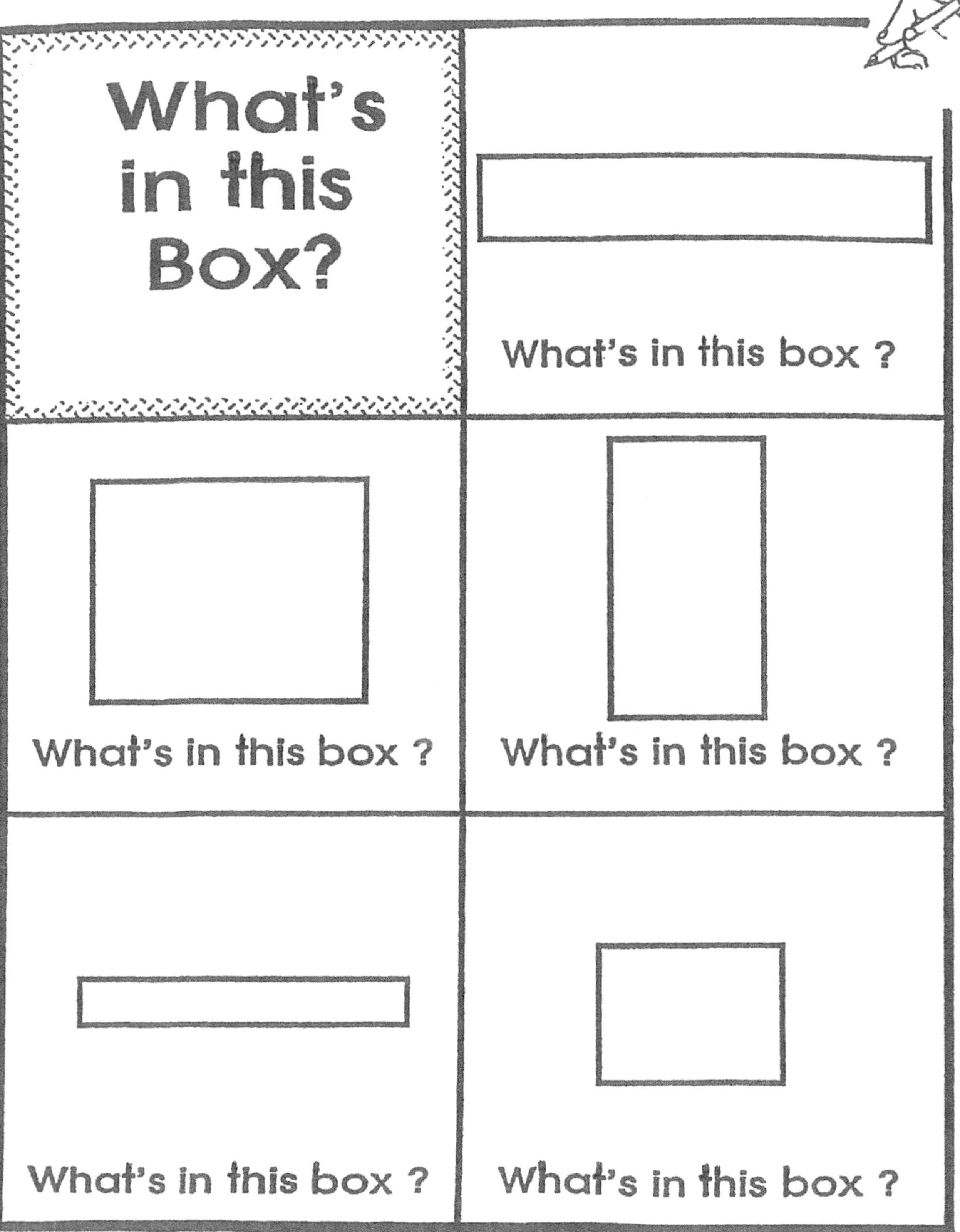

What's in this Box?
What's in this box ?
What's in this box ?
What's in this box ?
What's in this box ?
What's in this box ?

in

Draw pictures for in.

in

<table>
<tr><td colspan="2" align="center">Draw a picture of the Preposition</td></tr>
<tr><td align="center">in the car</td><td align="center">in the house</td></tr>
<tr><td align="center">in the tree</td><td align="center">in my pocket</td></tr>
<tr><td align="center">in my mouth</td><td align="center">in your desk</td></tr>
<tr><td align="center">in the bag</td><td align="center">in the morning</td></tr>
</table>

on

on

Draw a picture of the Preposition	
on the table	on the T.V.
on the bus	on a plane
on your birthday	on your face
on Saturday	on top of

under

under

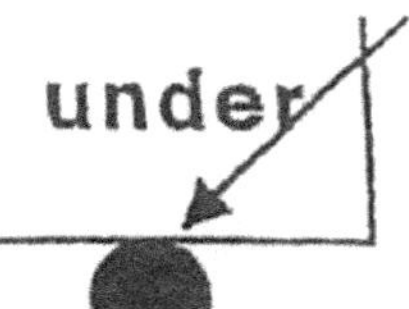

Draw a picture of the Preposition	
under the car	under the bridge
under the apple tree	under the ground
under the table	under the water
underneath the street	underneath my house

up

Read and Explain

1. Look up.

2. Stand up

3. Get up.

4. Go up there.

5. Go up the street.

6. Tie up your shoes.

7. She put her hair up in a ponytail.

8. Clean up this mess.

9. Go up the elevator.

10. Go up the escalator.

11. Go up the stairs.

12. Pick up the papers.

13. Make up a story.

14. I wake up at 7 o'clock.

Paper plus Oil = Transparent

1. Color your butterfly.

   Use bright markers.

2. Cut it out.

3. Lay it on top of a big paper.

4. Put 5 drops of oil on the butterfly.

5. Rub the oil into the paper.

6. Wipe off the extra oil.

7. Your butterfly is transparent.

down

upside down

Grass Can Harry

1. Get an empty soup can.
   Take the label <u>off</u>.

2. Cover the can <u>with</u> a light colour of
   construction paper.
   Glue <u>on</u> eyes, nose and a mouth.

3. Add arms by gluing a long strip of paper
   <u>across</u> the back. Then add legs by gluing
   2 long strips <u>to</u> the bottom of the can.

4. Add potting soil <u>to within</u> an inch or 3cm
   of the top.

5. Spread grass seeds <u>all over</u> the soil.
   Then cover lightly <u>with</u> a final layer of soil.

6. Discuss that seeds need sun and water
   to grow.

7. Put the cans <u>on</u> a window sill or <u>on</u> a table
   <u>by</u> the sunlight.

8. Check for growth every day.
   Add water as necessary.

9. Measure the hair (grass) length.

beside

beside

Draw pictures for beside.

behind

Behind the Door Activity 

1. Preparation: The teacher uses an exacto knife to slice open the door pictures on 3 sides.

2. Students look for a large picture that they like in a magazine. They cut it out and glue it <u>in the middle</u> of a piece of construction paper.

3. Students glue the door <u>on top of</u> the picture and press open the door to see their picture.

4. Students give their papers to the teacher to staple as a book, and to read to the class.

* Student pictures be a either a place or a thing.

behind the door

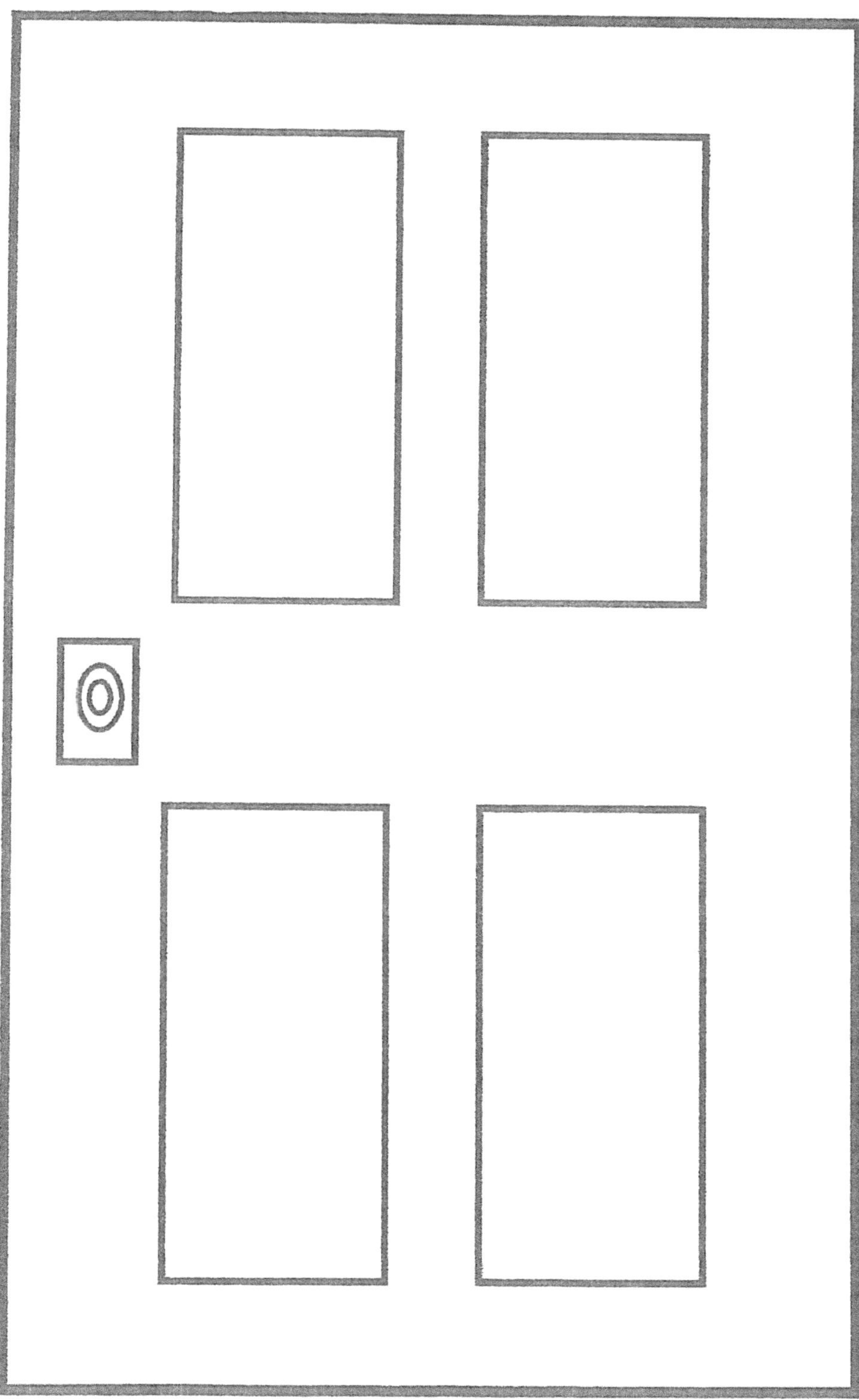

behind

Draw a picture of the Preposition	
behind me	behind the house
behind the trees	stand behind me
Sit behind me.	hide behind
behind the door	Look out behind you.

between

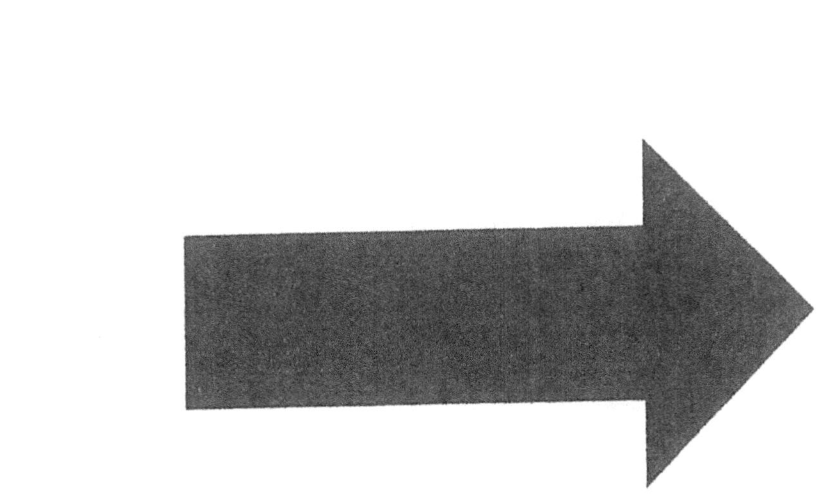

right

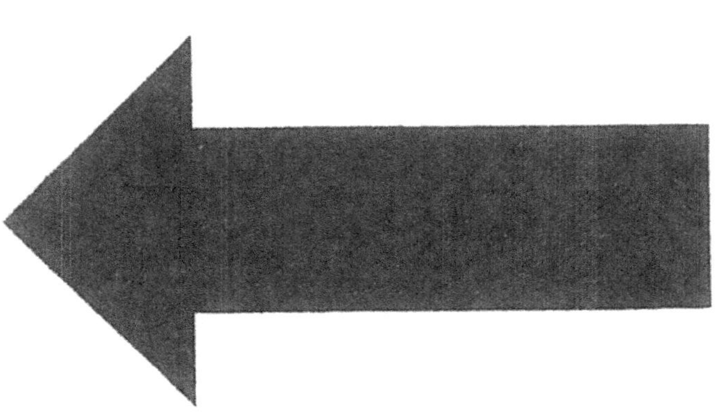

left

through

2 'I Spy' Activities

Give students a copy of a **Hidden Objects** page.
If you can, project it onto your Whiteboard.

Students have to find certain objects that appear in the picture as another students explains where the secret object.

The student who takes the lead must use prepositions to describe its position in relation to the other objects.

The classmates must guess which object it is based on the clues.

The person who first identifies the correct object gets to describe the next one for the class.

Binoculars

Use toiler paper rolls to make pretend binoculars and then have students look through them to say, "I spy' sentences.
See how to do it on the next page.

through

Draw a picture of the Preposition	
through the tunnel	through the window
through the forest	through the binoculars
look through your backpack	flying through the clouds
walk through the garden	through with my homework

Spinners

Students love to create spinners and use them with other students. The spinners must be copied onto sturdy card stock so they will actually spin – you don't want it bending out of shape after 2 spins.

Students will fill in the sections with compliments, adjectives, future forecasts, Valentine's sayings, etc.

You can make a spinner with alphabet letter to spell our words or to say a word that starts with a letter.
You can write curriculum questions or to define terms.

Students will outline the spinner sections using colors and markers after the written work is completed.

If possible, laminate the spinners after or have students cover theirs with clear, tacky paper from the Dollar Store.

Students ought to show their final work to the rest of the class.

Required Vocabulary
through   on top   beside   on   around   between

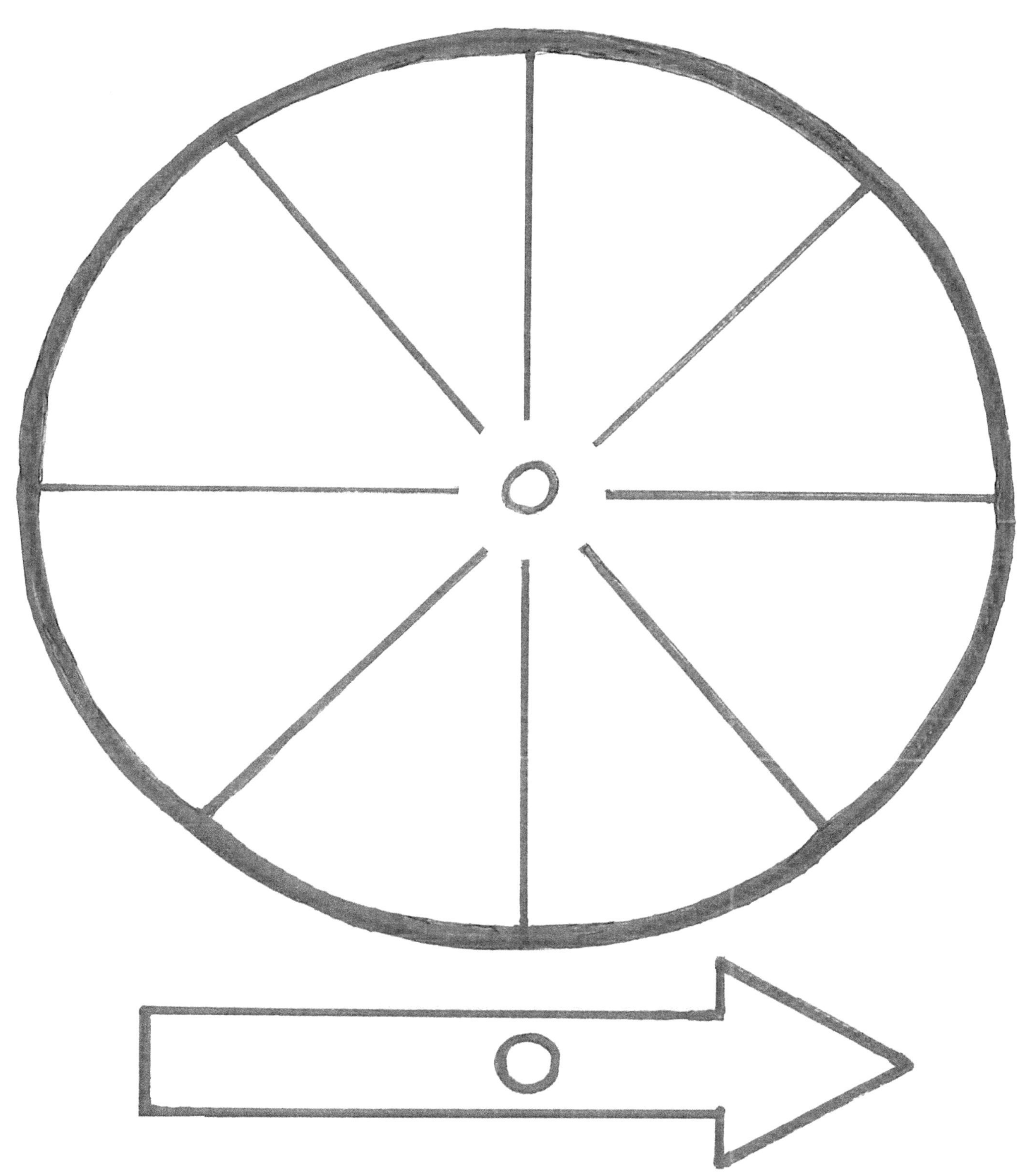

across

Draw a picture of the Preposition	
around the corner	around the pool
running around	looking around
around my head	stand around
ride around	stick around

MainStreams Publications
Copyright. 2002. Reproducible for Purchaser's Class
Where?
Prepositions
down
onto a planet.
12
In the rocket
1

under the sun
8
over the earth
5
behind the moon
10
through
the clouds
3

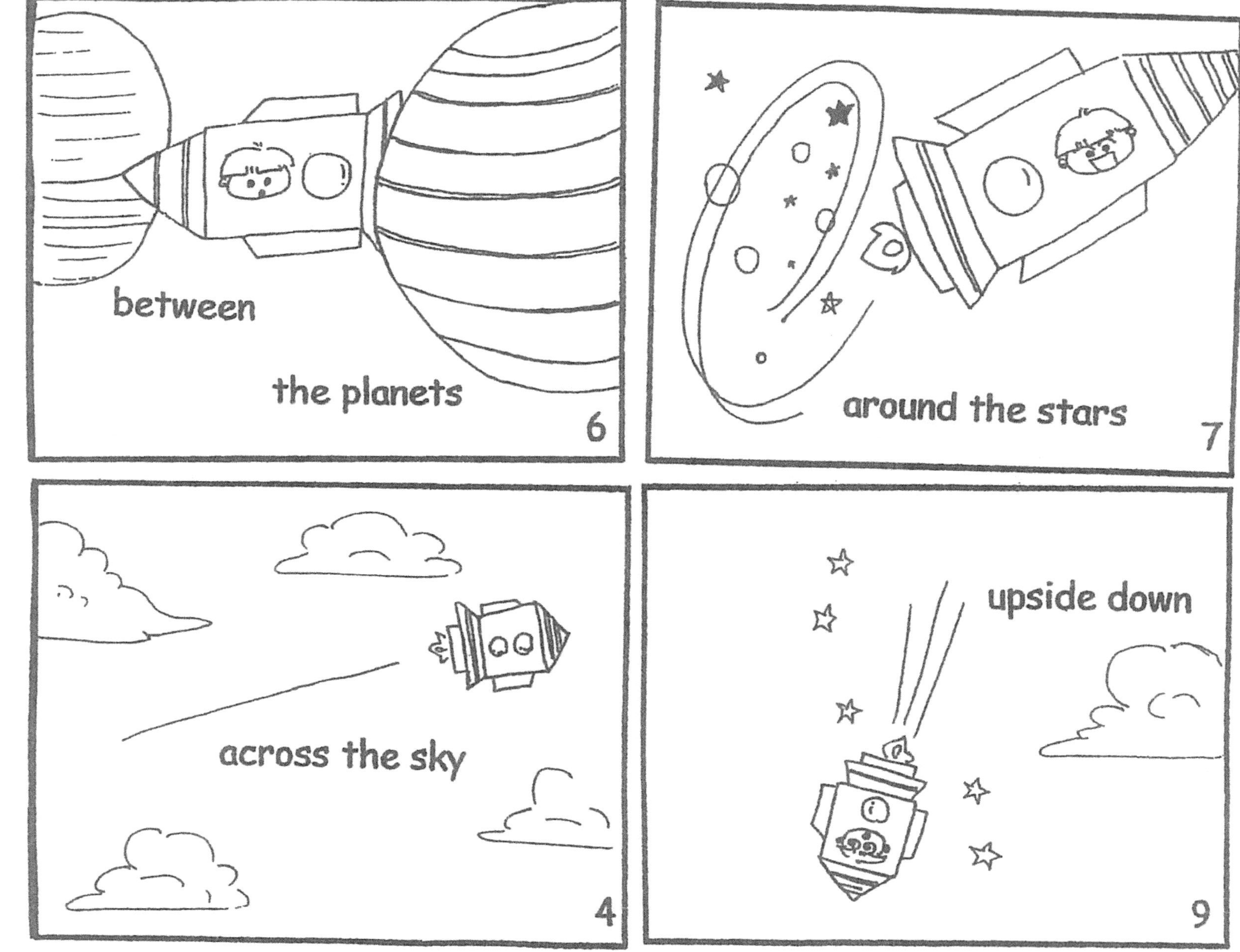

between
the planets
6
around the stars
7
across the sky
4
upside down
9

New Words

where
in   out   over   under
upside   down   up   into
hello   beside   behind   out
earth   moon   the   sun
through   on   across   sky
planets   between   around
rocket   stars   clouds

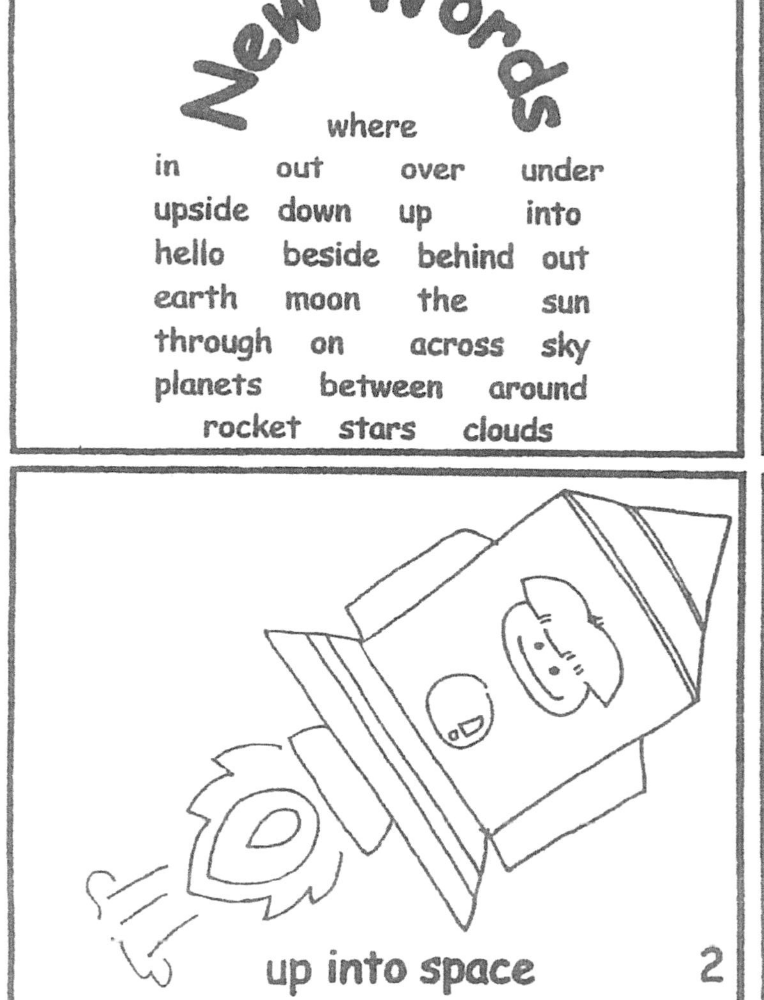

13

2

11

Preposition Simon Says

It's fun and easy especially after my students have been sitting too long. Simon Says is a great way to teach and review prepositions.

Students stand up and follow your instructions as they move hands and feet on, over, under, beside, between, etc.

You can change the name Simon to students' names, but if you say the name 'Peter', they are not supposed to move. Anyone that does, has to sit down. (Okay, be kind and give them 2 chances.) Start slow and then speed up.

The last person standing is the winner.

Sean says put your hand **under** your chin.
Linda says put your right foot **in front of** you.
Carlos says put your hands **behind** your back.
Teacher says put your finger **between** your eyes.
Peter says put your thumb **in** your mouth.

- over   - beside   - around   - onto   - in the middle
- on top of   - through   - upside down   - across

in the middle of

Draw a picture of the Preposition	
in the middle of my desk	in the middle of the pool
in the middle of your eyes	in the middle of the road
in the middle of the table	in the middle of the bed
in the middle of the boat	in the middle of the night

in front of

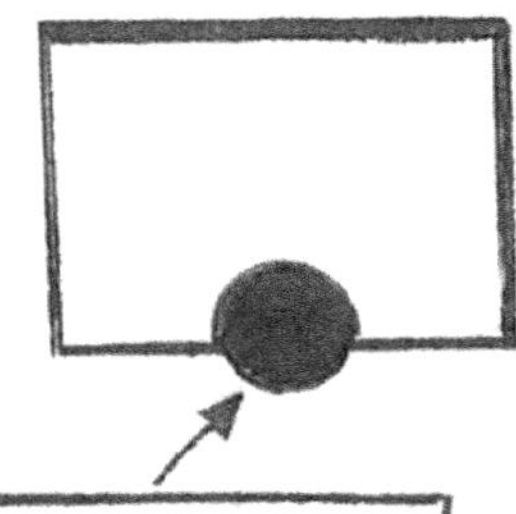

Draw a picture of the Preposition	
in front of the house	in front of the class
in the front seat of the car	in the front seat of the bus
on the front of my book	on the front of my tee-shirt
in front of the store	in front of the school

Movement with Prepositions – 4-5 Sessions

1. Chinese Ribbon Dance/Colored Streamers on Lummi Sticks

   a) Students can choose their own colors of bright crepe paper to tape on lummi sticks (raid the music room) and make beautiful streamers in the classroom.

   b) In the gym, allow the students to explore movement with the streamers. Then stop the class and ask specific students to demonstrate several interesting moves. Teachers may need to suggest moving ribbons above, around, behind, in front, figure 8s.

   c) After, ask students to work in unison with a partner. Ask several pairs to show their routine. Continue in pairs.

2. Choose a beautiful piece of instrumental music to play in class for students a day or so before taking it to the gym for the next ribbon class. Start the class again with individual movement, move into pairs, and finally allow partners to form groups of 4 or more with the task of choreographing a ribbon dance. Groups may be good enough to put on a show for other classes.

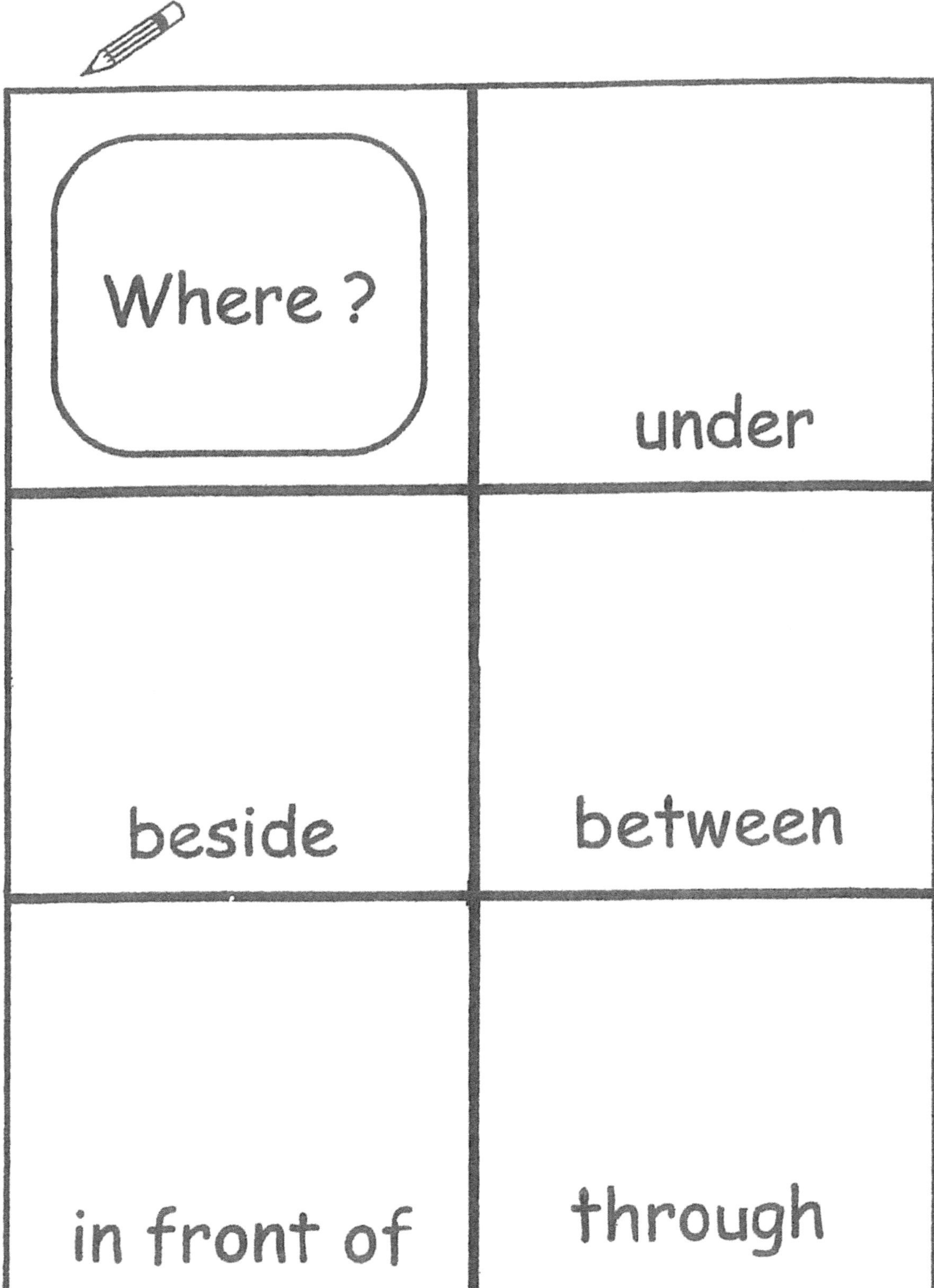

Where ?
under
beside
between
in front of
through

Where ?	in the middle
up	down
behind	over

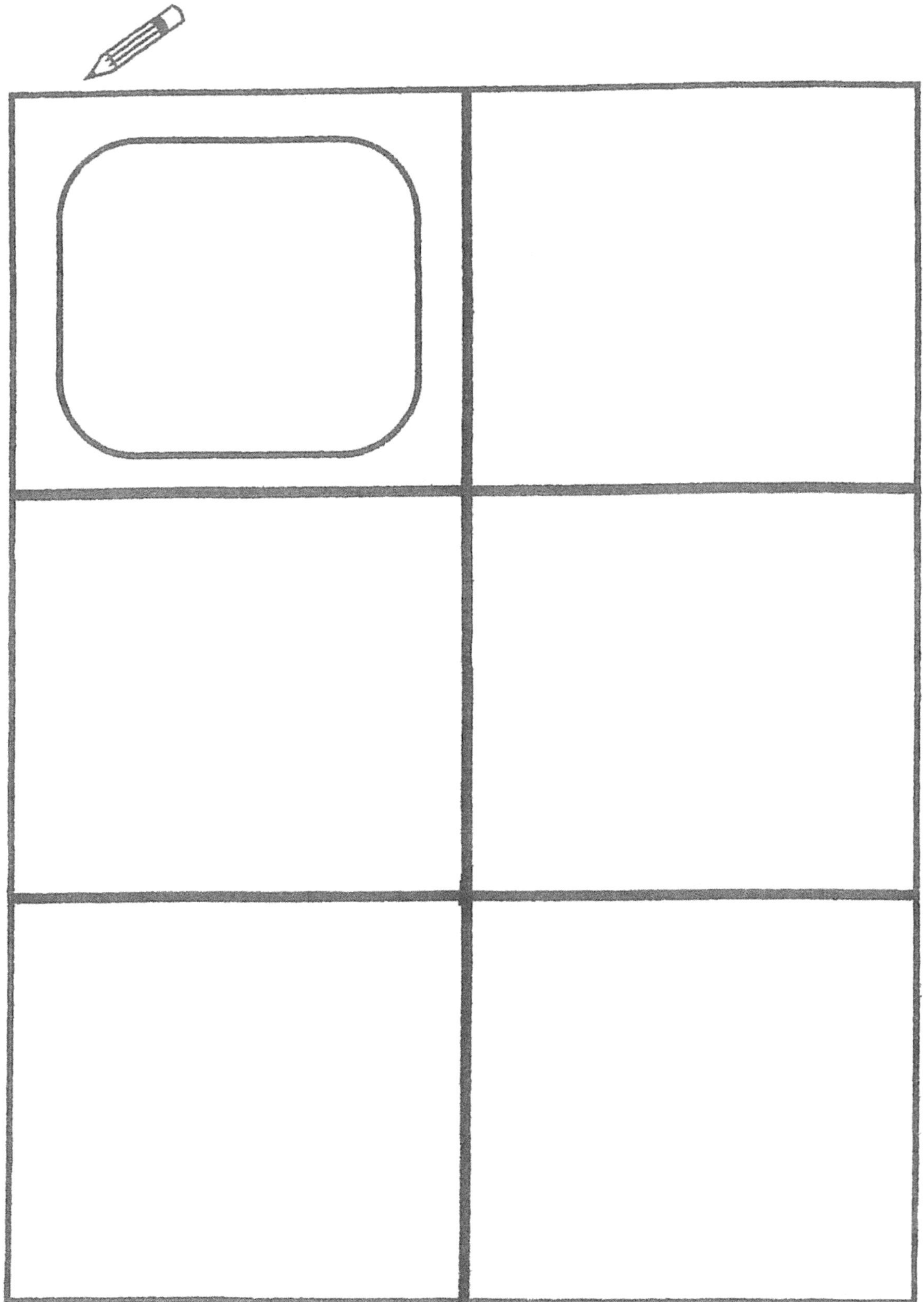

Prepositions Tell Where

1. Write where.

up the hill   down the hill   across the log

through the tunnel   behind the bushes

over the fence   under the fence

beside the train tracks   between the white lines

Students glue 4 copies of this tree onto a large construction paper, and then follow their teacher's instructions to show a tree for each season.
*add details such as weather, plants, etc.

Prepositions

Words that tell 'where' are named Prepositions. (Preh pŏ zi shuns)

in

on

under

over

beside

behind

between

in the middle

in the centre

through

across

in front of

to the right

to the left

at the bottom

at the top

off

Following Directions

1. Draw a river across the middle of your paper.

2. Draw a bridge across the river.

3. Draw a truck on the bridge.

4. Draw 2 houses below the river.

5. Draw a car between the houses.

6. Draw an airplane in the top right of the page.

7. Draw lightening coming through dark clouds.

8. Draw rain under the clouds.

9. Draw a hospital close to the river.

10. Draw an ambulance beside the hospital.

11. Draw a helicopter on top of the hospital roof.

12. Draw 2 cars on the left side of the page, but one car is upside down.

13. Draw somebody inside the car.

14. Write your name in the bottom right corner.

Where is/are my ____________ ?

In this activity students must guess where the teacher's objects are by using a prepositional phrase. Then they draw the object on their picture page.

1. Hand out the following drawing and identify the objects.

2. Tell students that you have lost or can't find something and they have to guess where it might be.

i.e., Teacher - Where did I put my book?
    Student – Is it under the sofa, beside the chair, etc

    Teacher - Where did I leave my glasses?
    Student – Are they between the cushions? Etc.

3. When the teacher decides the place is suitable, the students draw the object in that location on the page.

* You can use a made up picture drawing of your own another time or even have students draw up a location and play the game with the class.

* Try using the idea on a whiteboard, where a student has to come forward and draw the item. No paper used up!

Prepositions

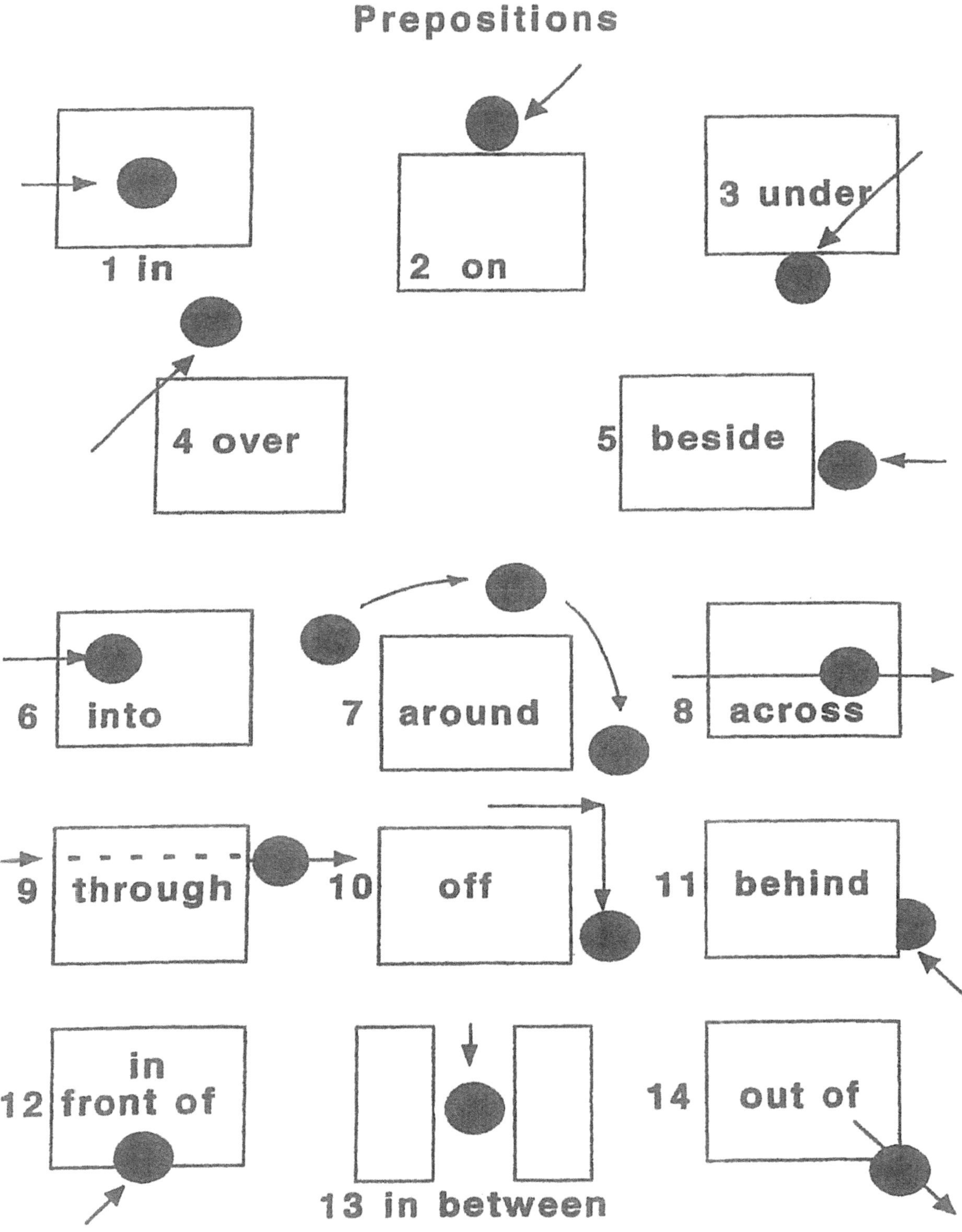

Why Bingo?

Bingo provides for an essential review of vocabulary as students have fun listening and helping each other find the right pictures.

Bingo requires active participation as students are engaged in looking, listening and identifying the appropriate picture.

Bingo lets the teacher enunciate each individual word carefully before extending language use by putting the word in context or a riddle, which is pretty tricky, but forces the kids to speak out.

Bingo allows the teacher an opportunity to assess student spoken language and pronunciation as they repeat the words and talk amongst themselves.

Use poker chips instead of Bingo chips
because they are bigger, more colorful and are not transparent.
If you can't find inexpensive poker chips then cut out multiple
small squares of colored stock card
or find something similar in the Dollar Store.

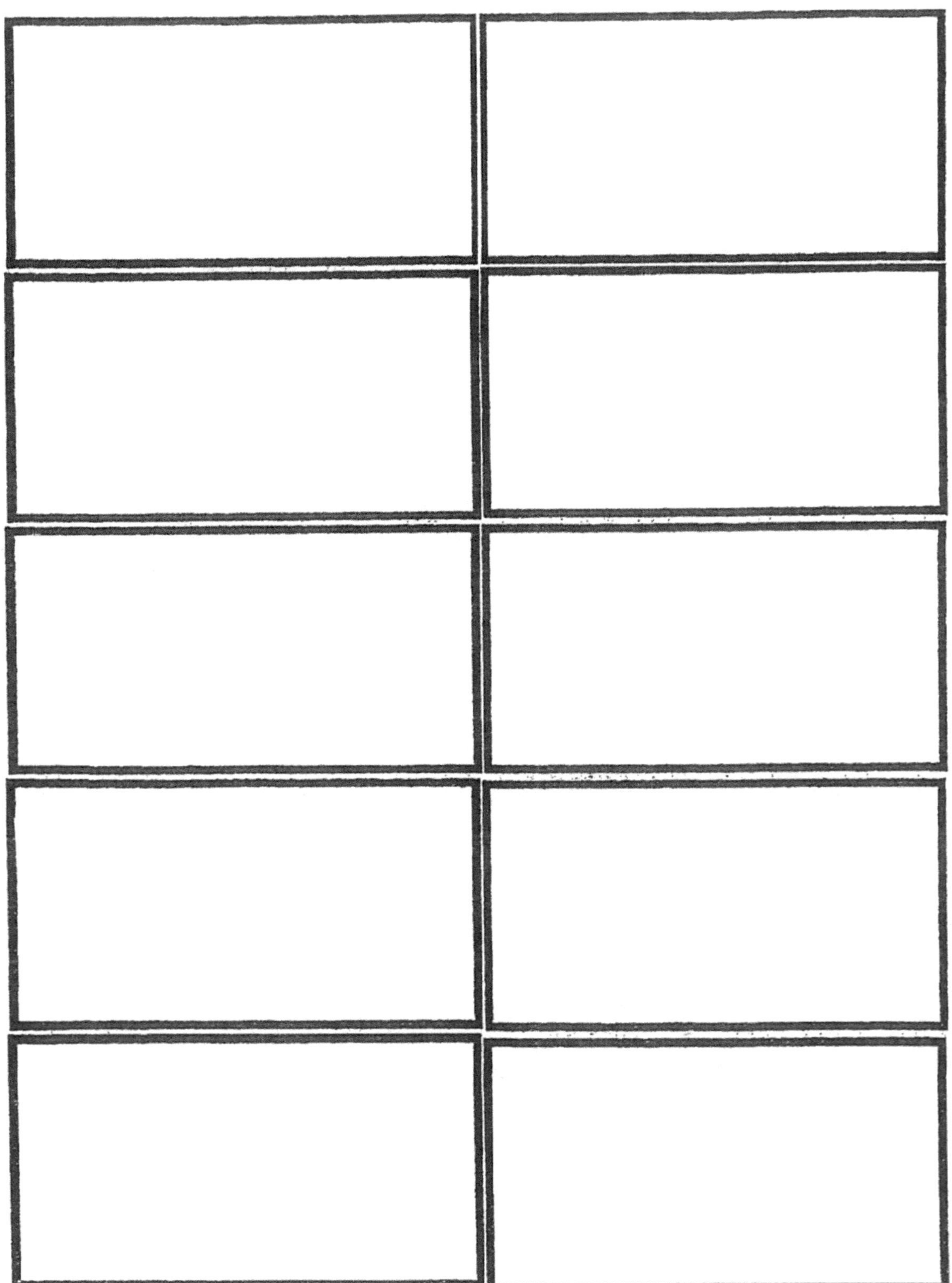

Prepositions Tell Where

Draw a picture and write an idea.

across the ________

across the ________

beside the ______

beside the ________

beside the ______

through the ____________

through the __________

behind the ______

behind the ______

behind the ______

Book Making

Here are 2 book-making ideas
where students practice using prepositional vocabulary.

1. Students create a book similar to the previous movie
   frame activity. They choose an object and have it go
   through activities that demonstrate prepositions.
   i.e., an ant moving places, a baby crawling places, etc

   Sing the song, 'On Top of Spaghetti' first and then hand
   out a copy of the song. Students draw a picture beside
   each prepositional phrase.

2. Easier than drawing a preposition story, this activity
   requires students to cut out magazine pictures then
   glue them on colored construction paper. They write
   the proposition on the page and staple all the pictures
   into a book. Show examples first especially funny ones.

Magazine Preposition Books 

Duration 5-6 Sessions

Skills – speaking, listening, reading, writing, and spelling of prepositional vocabulary

Collect magazines that students can use to cut out pictures. Ask your librarian for old science, wildlife, sports or teen magazines. You could also ask parents for suitable magazines. Fashion magazines do not generally have a variety of preposition pictures, and News magazines often show violent scenes – so you might want to exclude these kinds.

The Activity

1.   Start by showing students examples of prepositions that you cut from magazines and glued onto colored construction paper. The samples should have the word printed from a computer, and pasted under the picture.
*   Samples should be large, and colorful, even humorous. Your computer font and size should be large and clear. (size 18 or larger)

2.   Students should work in groups of 4. This number allows English language learners to hear the ideas of others, to speak comfortably at their level of English fluency, and to get help if needed. Teachers can ask group members to work on a book of their own, or to collect pictures as a group, in which case there shouldn't be duplicates.

3.   Students should save their pictures in their workbook or a file folder with their name, and cut pictures (2 days).

4.   Ask some students to show examples that are clear or humorous before students start cutting on the second day.

5.   Assign a day or time to paste the pictures on background paper.

6.   Students use the computer to type, spell check and print their words.

7.   Show and read the preposition books with each other in class.

<u>New Prepositions</u>

Teachers can introduce these new prepositions easily by focussing on simple contexts in day to day routines that also provide a review for students who already understand them.

1. Put your name <u>on the bottom</u> of the paper (or <u>on the top</u>).

2. Look <u>out of</u> the window and find something that is . . . .

3. Review Fire Drills with students for the preposition <u>out of</u> .

4. Lead a 4 minute class exercise and have students:

- reach <u>to the top of</u> the room, then <u>to the bottom</u>

- twist <u>to the left</u> then <u>to the right</u>, <u>left side</u> – <u>right side</u>

- wave your arms like a tsunami <u>through the air</u>, left to right

   and around again.

- put your palms together <u>in the centre of</u> your chest, and

   push together, then curl fingers together.

5. Introduce the next page of prepositions. Say and read.

   Lastly, compose sentences together for students to copy.

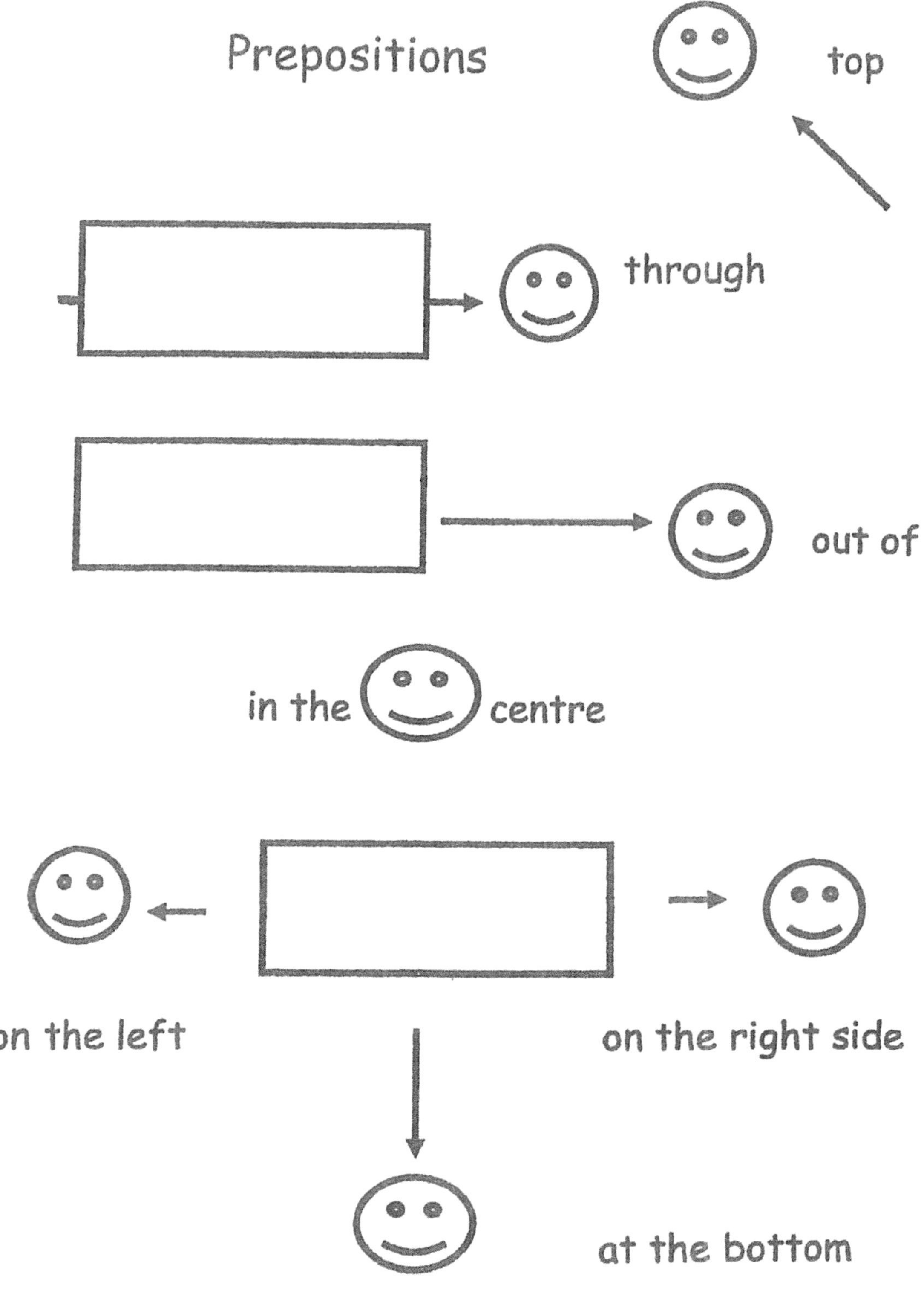

Prepositions
top
through
out of
in the centre
on the left
on the right side
at the bottom

Prepositions

1. Read and say these new prepositions.
in the middle of
in the centre of
at the bottom of
across the
on the right side of
on the left side of
on the right
on the left
in the corner
in the top right corner
in the bottom left corner
at the top of

2. On the back of this paper, draw 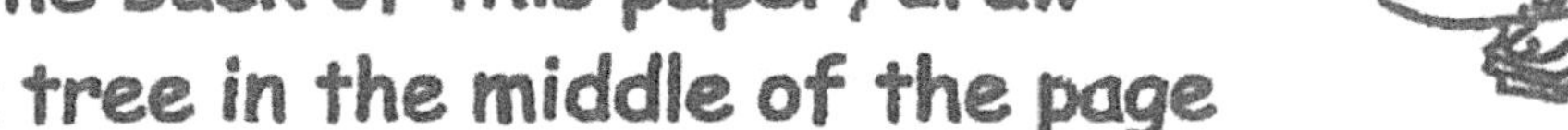
    - a tree in the middle of the page
    - a bird at the top in the centre
    - your name in the bottom right corner
    - a school on the right side of the tree
    - a store on the left side of the page
    - a street across the paper
    - a million dollars in the bottom left corner

go around

go down

to the right

go behind

go the center

go to the left

go under

beside

go to the bottom

over the hill

Ride back home.

Circle the Prepositions

1. My brother is on the swing.

2. Mother's coffee fell off the table.

3. The paper is under your desk.

4. The sports car was racing down the street.

5. Can you see up there?

6. What's that over there?

7. Come here and sit beside me.

8. Don't run across the road.

9. Why is the teacher   standing behind me?

10. I can't see if you stand in front of me.

11. Let's walk around the park.

12. You have to go through the doors and turn left.

The Dangerous Beach
Following Directions
(Prepositions)

Draw these.

1. Draw a blue line <u>across</u> the middle of your paper.
2. <u>Below</u> the blue line draw people swimming.
3. <u>At the top</u>, make a yellow sun.
4. Make a lifeguard chair <u>on the right</u>.
5. Draw a sandcastle <u>on the left</u>.
6. Make a brown line <u>across</u> the page and <u>between</u> the sun and castle.
7. <u>Under</u> the brown line, colour the sand light brown.
8. Put 2 sun umbrellas <u>on</u> the beach.
9. <u>Above</u> the brown line, make some grass.
10. Make a family <u>around</u> one umbrella.
11. Put an orange towel <u>beside</u> the other umbrella.
12. Make a starfish, jellyfish and a shark <u>under</u> the water.
13. Draw the lifeguard running <u>towards</u> the water, shouting, Get out, get out.
14. Make 4 seagulls <u>up</u> in the sky.
15. Draw an ice-cream, and pizza store <u>on</u> the grass.
16. Draw a child playing <u>with</u> a pail and shovel.
17. Draw a grey cloud <u>next to</u> the sun.

Scenic Art

A scenic picture will be used to cut out the foreground and background(s) which will then be layered with glue on a cardboard/sturdy backing. The results will be 3D lovely!

 Prepare an example(s) of the final product to show the class, and also to demonstrate the steps they will need to take.

1. Students will choose a fair-sized photo of scenery from either a calendar or a magazine. The photo ought to have a foreground and at least one background layer (hopefully more). Ensure that each student shows you his/her photo before they start. Is it easy enough to do with 3 layers or will it be too difficult?

2. Students cut along the layers, and glue the background down on the backing (either cardboard or heavy stock card).

3. The next layer is raised and positioned a wee bit over the background to show depth. That new layer is raised up beyond the background by using cardboard or even Styrofoam backing.

4. Students continue layering their photo sections until it is complete. Students trim around the edges and write their name on the reverse side.

Required Vocabulary – in back   in front   behind   over   onto
foreground   background   across   around   below   etc.

Obstacle Course in the Gym #2

In class, students will form a team and plan to create an obstacle course for a future gym time.

How
1. Students must know what equipment is available to use and then make a drawing of their plan. The team will decide how to use propositions in their instructions.

2. Next, the team will compose numbered instructions before typing them on the computer for other students to know what to do during the obstacle course.

3. The team must review the hard copy then hand it to the teacher for editing. Teams will then make any needed corrections.

4. Each team member will get a copy of their instructions and arrange to do a trial run themselves during gym time or after school. If all is well, then they sign up to do the course for others.

5. Teams may need to make changes to both their file and drawing before it is copied for the rest of the class.

Example
1. Start at the _____________.
2. Bounce the ball towards the pylons and then toss it back
    to the next student in line.
3. Run around the _________ etc. etc.

Preposition Activity
Obstacle Course in the Gym #1

The teacher plans a gym lesson where students use various equipment to demonstrate a preposition. i.e., students must walk across the bench, jump over the pylon, toss a ball into the hoop, etc. etc.

Be sure to use a variety of equipment.

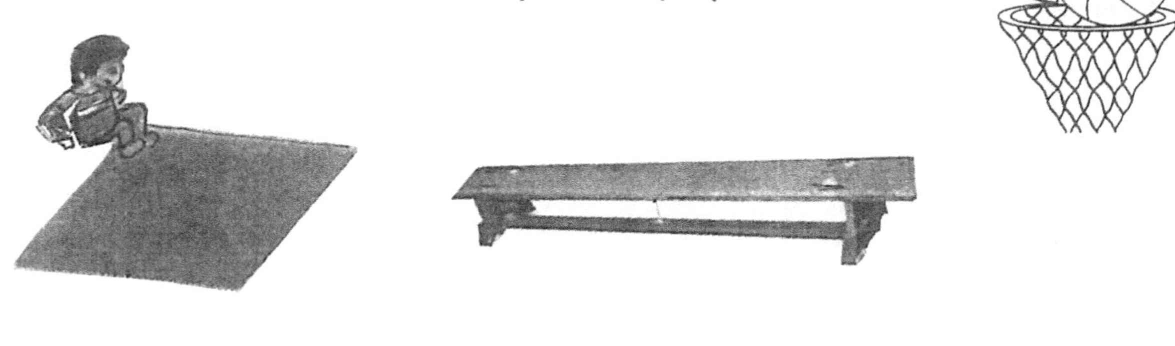

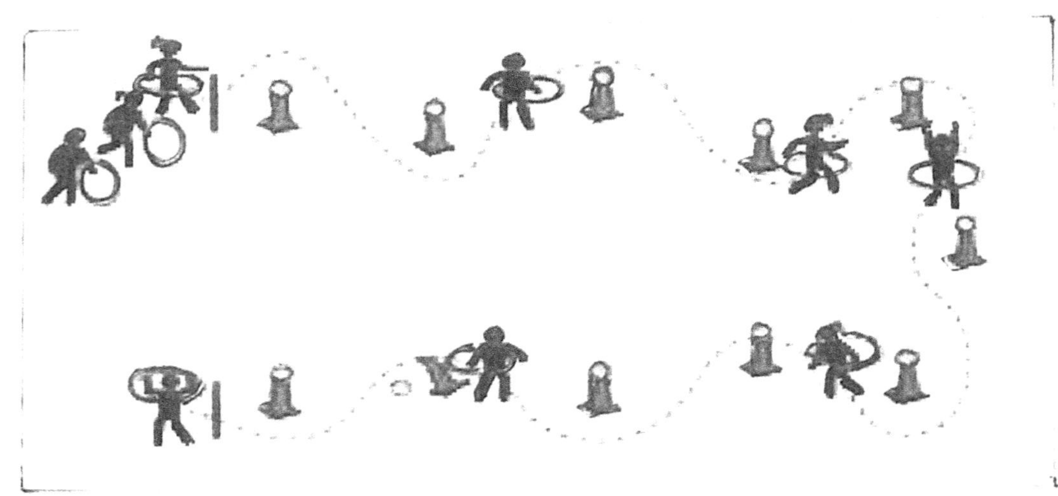

Following Directions

Use the picture of the bedroom for this activity.

1. Draw books on the middle shelf.
2. Hang your backpack on the hook.
3. Put your shoes under the bed.
4. Make a sun outside the window.
5. Put a rug beside the bed.
6. Lean a baseball bat against the wall.
7. Draw a poster on the wall.
8. Draw a CD player near the lamp.
9. Make the plug go across the floor into the socket.
10. Draw yourself under the blanket.
11. Put a clock on the dresser beside your bed.
12. Put some toys on the bottom shelf.
13. Draw some pens on top of your desk.
14. Draw a telephone beside the clock.
15. Put a globe on the top shelf.

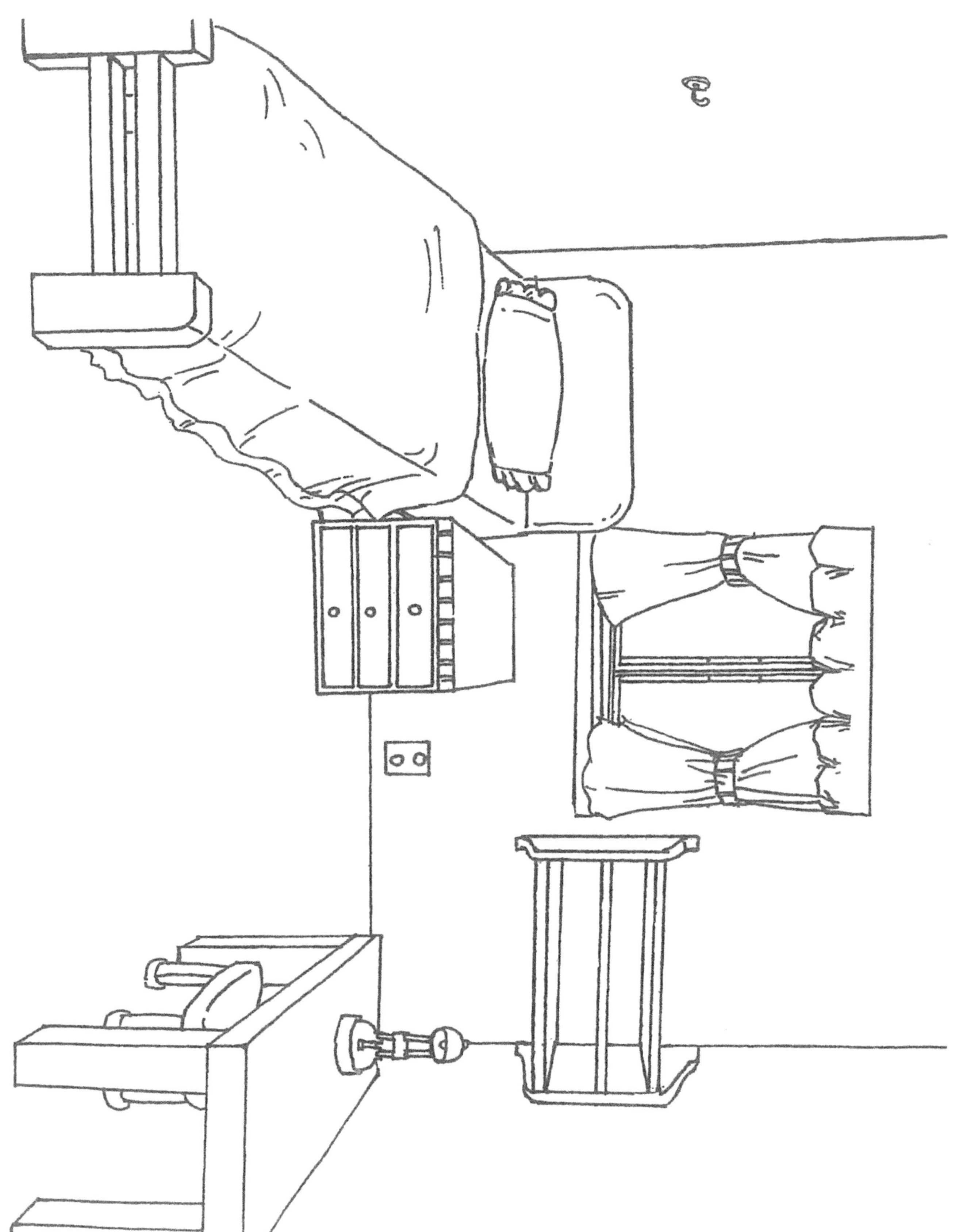

Following Directions

1. Draw stars around the moon.

2. Make the lightening go through a cloud.

3. Put hair on the guy's head.

4. Make your name on the banner.

5. Put the paper on a desk.

6. Draw a ruler under the desk.

7. Draw a poster on the wall.

8. Draw an arrow through the heart.

9. Make the grass under the tree.

10. Put the circle inside a square.

11. Put a dot in the middle of the circle.

12. Make another tree behind the first tree.

13. Draw some pens on top of the desk.

14. Draw a nose in the center of the guy's face.

15. Draw a pimple on his chin.

16. Colour the lightening yellow from top to bottom.

17. Write 100% on the paper.

18. Draw an eye and a mouth on the moon.

Prepositions

Following Directions

At the bottom, write your name.

On the right side, draw a big tree.

On the left side, draw a monster.

Draw big teeth inside the monster's mouth.

In the centre, draw a girl running toward the tree.

Underneath the girl, draw grass. Draw it across the paper.

Draw a baby monster in front of the big monster.

Draw a boy climbing up the tree.

Next to the tree, draw a small box. Draw a dog in the box.

Draw a helicopter above the girl.

Draw 2 men in a parachute jumping out of the helicopter.

In the background, draw a mountain.

On the mountain draw a tunnel.

Draw train tracks across the mountain.

Make the girl say, Come on. We'll be late for the train.

Following Directions

Follow these directions on a blank paper.

1. Make a small X <u>in the middle of</u> the page.

2. <u>In the top left corner</u>, make a large triangle.

3. Write your name in <u>the top right</u> corner.

4. Draw a circle <u>around</u> the X.

5. Put a square <u>in the middle of</u> the triangle.

6. Draw a line <u>through</u> the square.

7. <u>Underneath</u> the circle make another X.

8. Draw another X <u>on both sides of</u> the circle.

9. <u>On top of</u> the circle, make a red X.

10. Draw a line <u>across the bottom of</u> the paper.

11. <u>Below</u> your name draw a small diamond shape.

12. Draw a red frame <u>along the edge of</u> the whole paper.

13. <u>In the middle</u>, <u>at the bottom</u> make an oval (egg shape).

14. Make a straight line <u>from</u> the diamond half way <u>down</u> the page.

15. Put a red dot <u>on the left side</u> of the paper.

16. Make a red line go <u>around</u> the paper <u>next to</u> the shapes.

Following Directions

Follow these directions.

1. Make a tree on the left side of the paper.

2. Put a bird in the middle of the tree.

3. Draw a boy beside the tree.

4. Make grass under the boy's feet.

5. On the right, make a car.

6. In between the tree and the car, make a traffic light.

7. Make a kite over the tree.

8. Draw a string from the kite to the boy's hand.

9. Put yourself in the car.

10. Make a bear behind the tree.

11. Draw a squirrel climbing up the tree.

12. Draw two clouds above the traffic light.

13. Draw a line across the page, under the light.

14. Make a dog walking around the car.

15. Make a police officer in front of the car with his hand up to stop.

16. Draw a spider crawling through the grass.

17. At the top draw a sun with sunglasses.

18. At the bottom of the paper write your name.

**Your next assignment
is to draw your own picture,
and then write up directions for a partner to follow.**

A Fill in the Blanks Story

"Where's your owner?" Pat asked as he looked _______ at the puppy. The little dog was shaking all _______ so Pat spoke ___ it gently. The puppy whined. Maybe it was scared or hurt. Pat sat down __________ it and the pup wiggled the entire ___________ part of its body.

"Ah, you're friendly." said Pat. He looked _____________ at the damage from the hurricane and mumbled, "I guess you are all alone now."

The hurricane had come _________ the city and destroyed everything ___ its way. Most people had escaped the city early, but the puppy had been left ___________ by itself.

"You're okay now." said Pat, and as he stood ____, the puppy moved and leaned ___________ Pat's leg. "You're a good wee doggie. You're safe now. Come home _______ me."

Pat and the tiny pup walked _____________ his family's car together. When he got _________ his mom, Pat yelled. "Look what I found ________ all the rubble, mom."

He bent down and lifted the pup _______________________ him to show his sisters. It was love ___ first sight!

3-Frame Flip Books

In this activity, students choose a preposition of location and then illustrate the concept. It would be a good idea for the teacher to have an example of the flip book to show end result to the class. The 3 frames represent a subject, a preposition and a location.

Teachers copy the following frame on sturdy stock card.
Each student gets a copy of the 3-frame and cuts it out.
Teachers prepare many squares of paper that fit the ones in the 3-frame form.

How
The student writes a preposition clearly in the middle box.
The student staples an equal number of paper squares onto the top of 1st and 3rd squares. The pages will flip up – it's a flip book.

In the 1st square students write a person/animal on each separate paper square. i.e., My mother, the teacher, etc

On the 3rd square, students draw a place or location.
i.e., the road, the the tunnel, the hall, the bridge, etc.

The 3 squares taken together will form a sentence.
  i.e., My dog went <u>across</u> the road.
   The truck drove <u>across</u> the bridge.

Students share their flip books to each other and to the class.

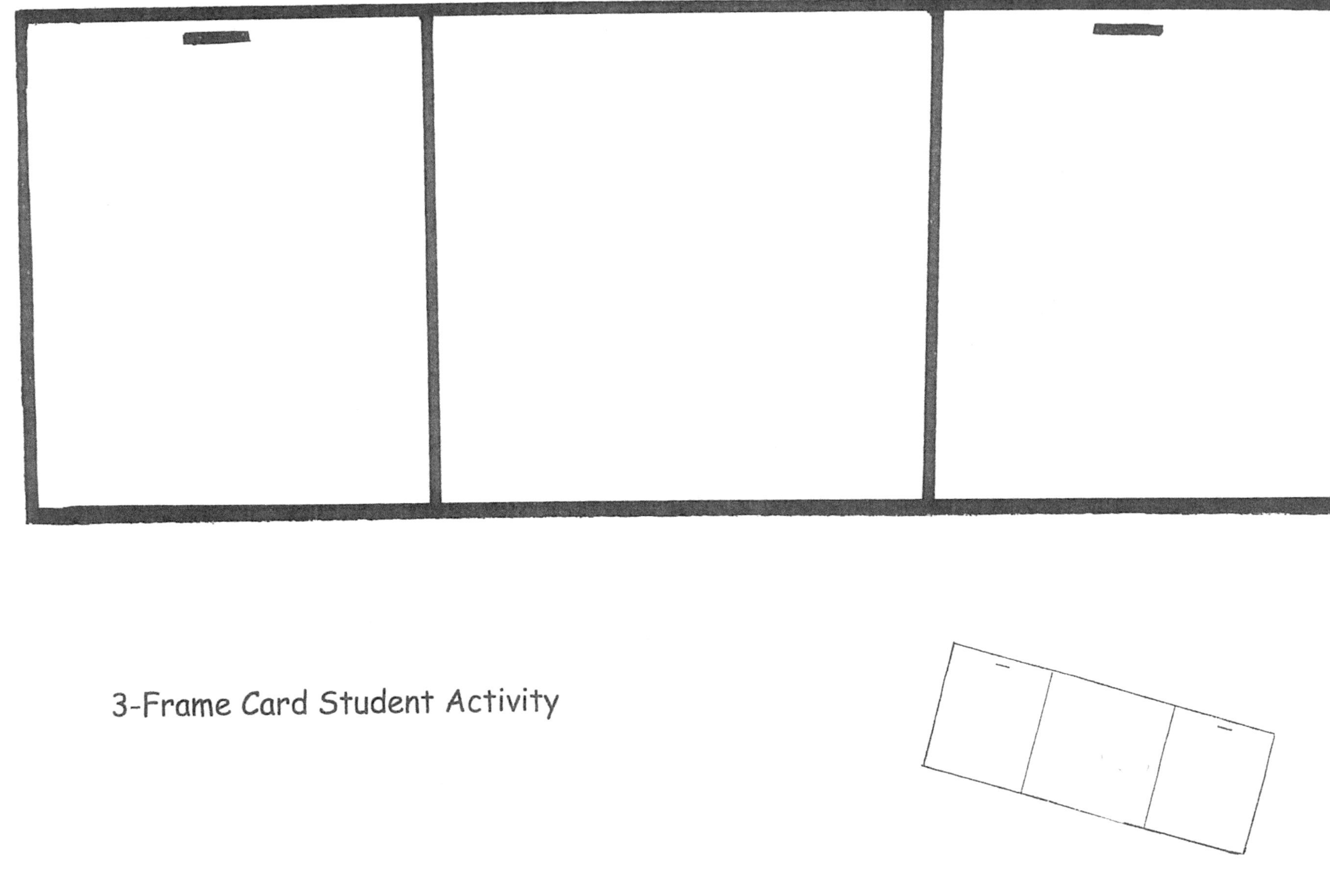

3-Frame Card Student Activity

WatchKnowLearn.org

Okay, this is not a game – but I just had to add it in case you weren't aware of it. WatchKnowLearn is a super-directory of over 50,000 free educational video links that are organized by subject matter.

You'll have to sign up on their website even though the service is free for teachers, parents and students everywhere.

Everything on the site can be translated into Spanish or Chinese by clicking the language button at the top right.

Rather than spend a lot of time clicking on the various subject areas, I went to the Search bar and typed in Compound Words first and then later I searched for Persuasive Techniques. Both times I was pleased with the range and quality of offerings. A great many had animation with text and voice or song overlay – all of which is attractive and fun for younger students. Why turn yourself upside down to get attention – just try a pertinent video.

1. Listen to the teacher read the prepositions.
2. Give a sentence with the prepositions.
3. Afterwards, choose one activity to work on with a partner.

* Prepositions of Place

in   on   over   above   under   beneath   beside
between   in   next to   near   by   in front of
at the top of   in the back   in the center/middle of

* Prepositions that Tell Direction

to   from   towards   across   around   into   through
across   outside   inside   off   against   below

* Prepositions that Help Tell When or Time

at   as soon as   before   until   since   until
before   after   in (month)   on (date/Special Day)
during   about   for (an hour/minute/seconds/weeks/years)

Choose one activity to do with a partner

- Write riddles for prepositions of time.

- Create a 'fill in the blank' test for prepositions of direction.

- Make a word search for prepositions of place.

What is a Preposition Phrase?

A prepositional phrase is a preposition plus a noun or a pronoun.

Examples,   Judy fell <u>down the hill</u>.   down . . . . the hill
                      Share the candy <u>between you</u>. between . . . you

Highlight the prepositional phrases.

1. I rode my bike up the street.

2. There is a bus stop in front of my house.

3. We had a vacation in Mexico.

4. His pen rolled off the desk.

5. Go up this street, and turn left.

6. The baseball flew over the fence.

7. Don't run across the road.

8. I put your stuff in your backpack.

9. I walked all around the store to look for you.

10. We went to the movies.

11. I sat behind my friend.

12. Come here and sit between us.

13. I can see over there.

14. Don't stand in front of me.

15. The subway is under the street.

Preposition Phrases

Finish writing these proposition phrases.

Your money is in _______________________________

His books are under _______________________________

The thief came through _______________________________

You are not allowed to go into_______________________________

Don't let the baby go outside_______________________________

He threw the ball over _______________________________

Look at that kid running across _______________________________

I had a holiday in _______________________________

I like to play video games on _______________________________

The fish jumped out of_______________________________

Draw a line in the middle of_______________________________

Write your name at the bottom of _______________________________

Let's roll down _______________________________

Sit next to _______________________________

The Little Spider

<table>
<tr><td>Baby spider goes across his web in the tree.</td><td>It's such a little spider. No one sees it go down the tree.</td></tr>
<tr><td>Baby spider goes through the long green grass.</td><td>It goes over a hill and then sees the garden. How nice !</td></tr>
<tr><td>Spider goes in and out of the flowers – all around.</td><td>Little spider thinks this is a nice place to live, so it spins a web between the flowers.</td></tr>
</table>

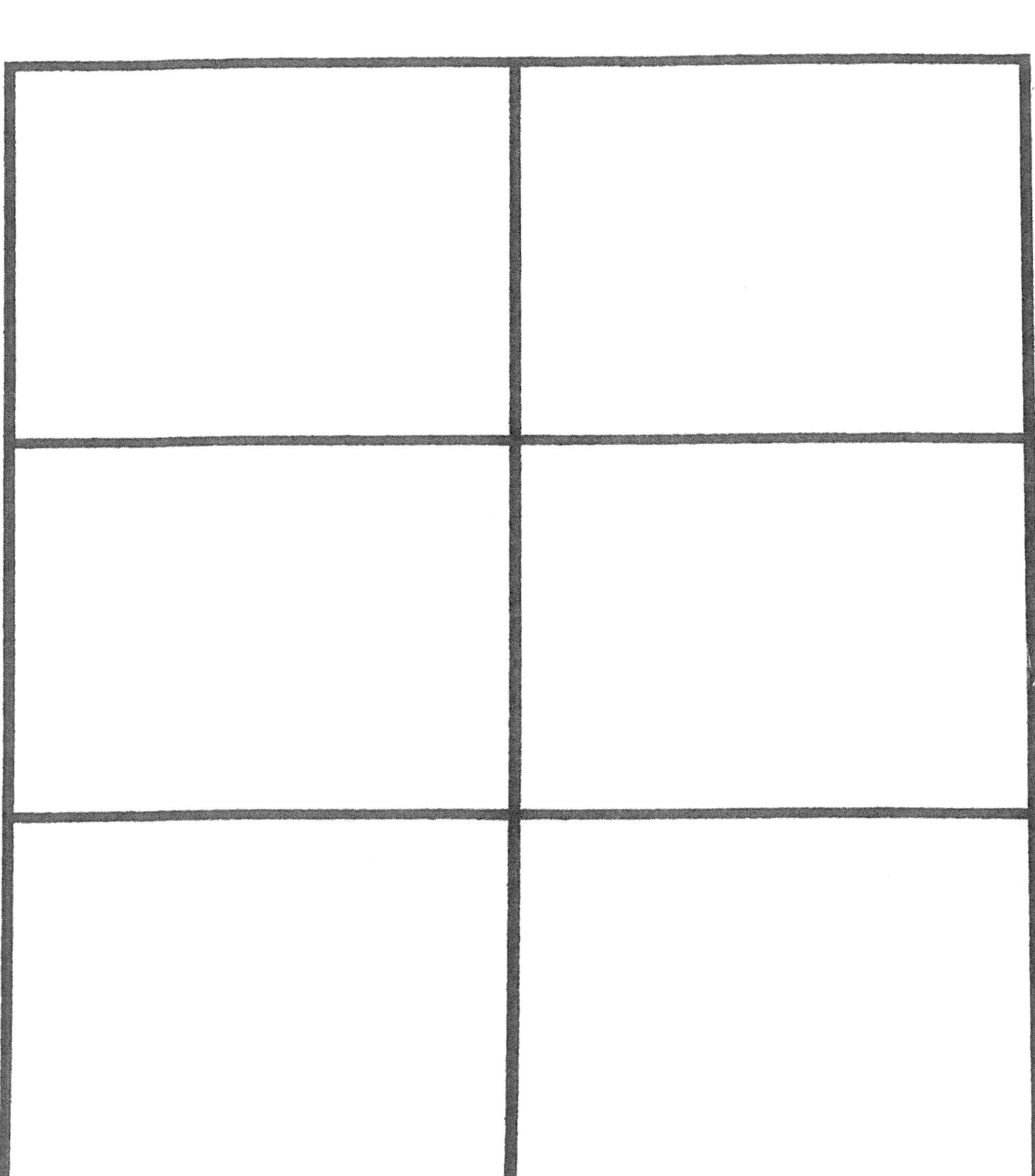

Use for Time Lines/Plot Development/Sequence

The Trip

Use the movie frames to draw this story.

Frame 1. An airplane is taking off the runway.

Frame 2. It flies across the sky.

Frame 3. It flies up above a mountain.

Frame 4. It goes through clouds.

Frame 5. Then it flies over a country.

Frame 6. The plane descends onto the tarmac.

Frame 7. The luggage cart drives towards the plane.

Frame 8. The stairs go up against the door on the plane.

Frame 9. You come down the steps.

Frame 10. You have a big smile on your face.

Mom's Lost Keys

My mother is always in a hurry. She always runs around the house trying to get everything done and get everybody else ready in the morning. On Friday, my mom went crazy because she forgot where she put her car keys.

She asked everybody," Did you see my car keys?"
"Are they on the table? Are they in your pocket? Are they under the table? Are they next to the books? Are they over there? Are they behind the sofa? Help me look around the house everybody. I need to find my keys."

So everybody had to look around the house, under the beds, in shoes, over tables, under chairs, inside pockets, through the papers, along the hall, between the books, in front of the door, behind the TV, next to the coats, in the middle of the floor.

Now, you ask, where did my mom leave her car keys?
In the car!

Prepositions

Prepositions also tell when.

at 6 o'clock

for 2 days

since last week

in 1 hour

in the summer

on Monday

before Friday

soon

after

What is a Preposition?

Also, a preposition tells when, like a time or a day.

at	on	around	past	since
before	after	about		during
for	by	next	from	with

Read these examples

At 3 o'clock	at dinner time	at recess
On Friday	on the first day	on Monday night
Past 12 o'clock	past time for gym	half past two
By 9 o'clock	by Saturday	by dinner time
Next week	next Sunday	next time
after 7:00	after school	after the summer
about 2 hours	about 2008	about 5 weeks
since Friday	since lunch	since 6:30

Prepositions Also Tell When

Finish these examples of 'when' prepositions.

1. On Friday, on______________ , on ______________

2. On March 11, on ________________, on ________________

>   'on' is used with exact days and dates

3. Next month, next ______________, next ________________

4. At 9 o'clock, at ________________, at ________________

5. At lunch, at ________________, at ________________

>   'at' is used with exact times

6. In September, in ________________, in ________________

7. In the spring, in the ______________, in ________________

8. In 2006, in ____________, in ____________, in ____________

9. In the morning, in ________________

>   'in' is used with months, seasons, and years

10. For 2 weeks, for ________________, for ________________

11. For 20 minutes. for ________________, for ________________

Tricky Prepositions

1. These two prepositions are tricky.   **for**   **since**

2. Use 'since' when you talk about a start date or time.
   since 4 o'clock, since 2002, since Friday, since he left

3. Use 'for' when you talk about an amount of time.
   for 2 hours, for a month, for 5 years, for now

4. Write the correct preposition.

a) I've been here _______________ 8 o'clock.

b) I'm going to New York ____________ 7 days.

c) He's played soccer _____________ 2004.

d) We read quietly _________ a whole hour.

e) She practices piano _____________ an hour every day.

f) She has studied piano _______________ she was a little girl.

h) Can I stay at his house ____________ the night?

i) I've been a genius _______________ I was born.

j) You've been watching T.V. ____________ you woke up.

k) I held my breath ____________ one minute, forty-five seconds.

Prepositions

Listen, read and then write a sentence.

for

1. What are you looking <u>for</u>?
2. This is <u>for</u> my mom.
3. I need a Kleenex <u>for</u> my nose.
4. We have to wait <u>for</u> another hour.
5. It costs $2. <u>for</u> 5 apples.

___

of

1. I want <u>a bag of</u> chips.
2. Can you carry this <u>box of</u> books?
3. The cake is <u>made of</u> flour, eggs, sugar and oil.
4. <u>Take care of</u> your baby brother, OK.
5. Order 4 <u>cans of</u> pop with the pizza, please.

___

with

1. I want to come <u>with</u> you.
2. He's going <u>with</u> his mom.
3. She's playing <u>with</u> a friend.
4. I need to make a salad <u>with</u> dinner.
5. I forgot to bring my lunch <u>with</u> me.

___

to

1. Give this <u>to</u> mom.
2. He gave a Valentine <u>to</u> his girlfriend.
3. I'm going <u>to</u> the library.
4. We went <u>to</u> the pet store this morning.
5. I looked up at the sky to see the stars.

___

after
1. Where are you going <u>after</u> school?.
2. <u>After</u> this, I'm never going back..
3. That bully is running <u>after</u> me.
4. Let's get ice-cream <u>after</u> the movie.
5. <u>After</u> I finished my homework. I went outside.

---

at
1. We have to go <u>at</u> 5 o'clock.
2. He was <u>at</u> the soccer field all day.
3. I got this <u>at</u> the store.
4. I don't want to look <u>at</u> the dog poo.
5. I looked up <u>at</u> the sky.

---

next
1. I want to sit <u>next</u> to you..
2. He lives is <u>next</u> door to me.
3. I 'm <u>next</u> in line.
4. OK, you're <u>next</u>.
5. I want to go to the beach next time.

---

before
1. Let's go <u>before</u> it gets dark outside.
2. I need to finish this first <u>before</u> we go.
3. Brush your teeth <u>before</u> you go.
4. It's 10 minutes <u>before</u> 3 o'clock.
5. I took swimming lessons <u>before</u> I went sailing.

Prepositions of Time

Make a sentence for these prepositions of time.

since ____

for ____

about ____

at ____

past ____

by ____

on ____

during ____

after ____

before ____

around ____

from ____

next ____

Preposition Meanings

Read these prepositions and the meanings

1. Get out.   = Leave

2. Let's get out of here.   = Go

3. Get out your math book.   = Put the book on the desk.

4. Take out your math book.   = Put the book on the desk.

5. Take out the garbage.   = Bring the garbage outside.

6. Look out!   = Danger possible. Be careful.

7. Watch out!   = Danger possible. Be careful.

8. Find out.   = Learn the answer.

9. Pick out what you want.   = Choose something you want.

10. The teacher ran out of paper.   = no more paper

Please Look

A) What do they mean?
   Write a sentence as an example.

1. look after ____

2. look at ____

3. look out ____

4. look out for ____

5. look up ____

6. look into ____

7. look down on ____

8. look over ____

B) Write the correct meaning from the above list.

1. review the information _______________________

2. be careful _________________________________

3. find in the dictionary _______________________

4. watch the baby ____________________________

5. see out the window _________________________

6. investigate ________________________________

<u>Must Have Prepositions</u>

These English verbs <u>go with</u> these prepositions.
Read them. Write a sentence to practice.

1. play with _______________________________

2. proud of   _______________________________

3. borrow from _______________________________

4. surprised at_______________________________

5. apologize to_______________________________

6. pointing at_______________________________

7. worrying about_______________________________

8. belong to _______________________________

9. listen to _______________________________

10. remind you about _______________________________

11. married to _______________________________

12. blame it on _______________________________

13. agree with _______________________________

14. different from _______________________________

15. stand next to _______________________________

16. get out_______________________________

Treasure Island Maps
Skills: listening, following and giving directions. Speaking

Give each student a Treasure Island map sheet. Do not cut it out. Students must listen to your directions and draw what you ask.

After this activity students can drench the paper with tea water and cut it out when it's dry. Watch the Swiss Family Robinson video and read several pirate stories about women/men pirates.

1. Draw a compass in the top right corner of the paper.
2. Turn the paper sideways.
3. Draw a large green oval – this is the island on the treasure map.
4. Now, turn your paper back (vertical). At the bottom left, draw a pirate ship anchored in the water, near the island.
5. Next, draw 4 volcanoes in the middle of the island.
6. A river runs down from one volcano. Draw a blue line starting at the volcano and running to the SW of the island by the ship.
7. Draw 2 sharks to the left of the ship.
8. Draw a swamp in the NW of the island. Put an alligator in it.
9. Draw a forest along the East side of the island but leave a sandy beach.
10. On the beach draw 3 huts where people live. Add a fire in the middle.
11. Make the dark opening of a cave on the side of one volcanic mountain.
12. Draw a waterfall coming from half way down another mountain.
13. In the SE corner of the island, draw a rocky coast with waves splashing.
14. Along the west coast, draw trees with coconuts, bananas and mangos.
15. Add a snake, a tiger, a monkey, a goat, a turtle wherever you want.
16. Color your island and add any extra things you think of.
17. On the back of your island make an X where your treasure is hidden.
18. Dunk the paper in tea or coffee water. Then dry it and cut out your map.

Students trade maps and follow directions to locate each others treasures. The starting point is always the ship on the SW.

Prepositions with Compasses and Orienteering

1. Access a class set of compasses from an Outdoor Education department or Physical Education department. Draw a standard cross compass on the board and introduce the word, along with the N-S-W-E points. Use the proper prepositions and finally elicit from students if possible the compass point names for NW-NE-SW-SE. Have students explore the use of the compass and find true north.

2. Ask the same department for in-class orienteering activities for graph paper. In such activities students start from a defined point on the graph paper, follow the compass directions with their pencils, and end up with a picture of something; a horse, an object, etc. Allow students to try a new graph paper orienteering activity with a partner.

3. Invite a specialist(s) from the prior departments to come in and work their magic with your class.

www.ingramcontent.com/pod-product-compliance
Lightning Source LLC
Chambersburg PA
CBHW080519030726
47592CB00012B/3409